YOU CAN BE AN ENTREPRENEUR TOO!

A Kid's Guide to Starting a Business

YOU CAN BE AN ENTREPRENEUR TOO!

A Kid's Guide to Starting a Business

Dr. Anthony Clark, PhD

This book may be ordered through booksellers or by contacting:

iGlobal Educational Services, LLC
PO Box 94224
Phoenix, AZ 85070
www.iglobaleducation.com
512-761-5898

You Can Own a Business Too! *A Kid's Guide to Starting a Business*

ISBN-13: 978-1-944346-44-7

$$

DEDICATION

To Brendan, Abed, and Mamoun...three young entrepreneurs who are doing great things in the world.

$$
ACKNOWLEDGEMENTS

I also want to thank Surendra Gupta for his creativity in formatting and Dr. Anthony Clark for writing this book to help kids learn about business.

$$

CHAPTER 1
Business Is All Around You

You do business every week, and maybe most every day. That's right—*you* do a lot of business.

Business happens when people trade money for goods and services. When you buy a pack of gum from the grocery store, you're doing business. When your grandparents give you money for your birthday and you use it to buy a new toy, that's business. If you've ever sold lemonade on the side of the street, you've done business.

Goods and Services

Goods are things, or physical objects, consumers buy from businesses. Cars are goods. Couches, clothes, toys, and candy bars are all goods. You can probably think of thousands of goods that you and your family members buy every year.

Most people also spend a lot of money on **services**. Hair cutting and styling is a good example of a service. Lawn mowing is a service. When someone goes to the doctor, he's paying for a service.

Goods and Services (contd)

Some companies only sell goods and other companies only sell services. However, a lot of businesses offer both goods and services. For example, many hair stylists sell shampoos, conditioners, and hair gels. Veterinarians offer services—they'll treat your sick dog, cat, or bird. But most vets also offer some goods for sale, such as special food and supplements for dogs and cats. See if you can think of some businesses that sell both goods and services.

Without business, people would have a hard time getting all the things they want and need. If there were no business being done in the world, we would all have to make everything on our own. Can you imagine having to make your own cereal, your own cereal bowl, and your own spoon? Without business, you and your family would have to make all of your own food, your own clothes, your own furniture, and your own house!

Wants and Needs

We all have wants and needs, and sometimes people get the two confused. Young people most often confuse these two, but even older people get them mixed up at times. **Needs** are things, goods and services, that you can't really live without. Food is a need for sure—without at least some of it, you won't be alive very long. Housing, or shelter, is another need. While it's true that some less fortunate individuals live

Wants and Needs (contd)

a long time without having a real house or apartment, most people would agree that housing is a need. Clothes are also a basic need. Of course, fancy or expensive clothes aren't a need, but people need some clothing in order to live a regular life.

Wants are things we don't really need to live life, but they do make life nicer. Transportation may be a need for some people because they have to get to work or school. But a flashy sports car, like a Porsche or a Ferrari, would be a want. A new video game system would also be a want; it may make your life nicer to have it, but you won't die without it.

Consider walking around your house or apartment with a notepad, writing down objects you see and then noting which ones represent wants and which ones are needs. Then ask a grownup to go over your list with you. You may be surprised to learn that some items you thought were needs are really wants.

Business makes life easier for everyone. Instead of having to milk a cow every time you run out of milk, you can just buy more at the store. Imagine when you get older and start driving a car. You won't have to build your own car—you'll be able to buy one from a car dealer. If your car breaks down, you can fix it yourself, if fixing cars is something you like to do and know how to do. If you don't know how to fix cars, you can pay a mechanic to fix it for you (which, of course, is what most people do).

People who do business as a way of making money are called **businesspeople**. Some businesspeople work for **companies**. There are millions of companies in the world of all kinds and sizes. McDonald's is a famous company. Wal-Mart is another famous company. You can probably think of lots of companies. You may pass several of them on your way to school every day. A daycare is a company. So is a bank. A carwash? That's a company, too.

Small Business vs. Big Business

Most businesses start as small businesses. Some of them grow into big businesses while others remain small forever. An organization called the **Small Business Administration**, also known as the SBA, has set up definitions for small businesses and big businesses. **Manufacturing firms—** companies that produce physical goods—with fewer than 500 workers are generally considered small. Businesses that aren't manufacturing companies and bring in less than $7.5 million per year in sales are usually considered small businesses. There are exceptions to these general rules, but they do give you an idea what makes a business small versus big.

If you look at the businesses in the town where you live, you'll probably find lots of small businesses and lots of big businesses. One isn't necessarily better than the other. Some very fine small businesses offer great products to their customers while providing an excellent income to their owners. In fact, some people prefer to do business with small, local companies.

People who own businesses are known as business owners or **stockholders**. Most big companies have lots of owners or stockholders. Most small companies are owned by a few people or just one person. If a few people own a company, the owners have what's called a **partnership**. If one person owns a company, that person is known as a **sole proprietor**. That's kind of a big word—*proprietor*. If you want to, it's fine to just call the person a business owner.

A **business manager** is a man or a woman who runs a company. Sometimes the owner of a business is also the manager. Sometimes the manager is paid by the owner to run the business. The top manager of a big company, or corporation, is called a **CEO**.

What is a CEO?

If you've paid much attention to the news, you've probably heard the term "CEO." It's a term that also comes up in movies from time to time. Some movies even portray CEOs as evil villains who want to dominate the planet. But most CEOs are not villains at all—they're just hardworking people who have done very well in business.

CEO is short for **chief executive officer**. The CEO is the big boss of a corporation. Some CEOs have become very wealthy, and some even become famous. Maybe you've heard of Bill Gates, who was the CEO of Microsoft for many years.

There are other titles that are common in corporations. The "COO" is the chief operating officer, or chief operations officer. The "CFO" is the chief financial officer. Many companies also have a "CIO," or chief information officer.

What is a CEO? (contd)

You probably won't come across these titles on a regular basis until you're a grownup working for a company yourself. But if you do hear about them, you'll at least have some idea what they're about. They all have very important roles in a corporation, and together—potentially along with some others—they make up a corporations' leadership team.

If you think you might want to be a businessperson one day, then this book is for you. You'll learn about what it takes to be a business owner. You'll find out where ideas for new businesses come from. You'll learn how to start planning a new business, how to find money to get it started, and how to let people know about your product.

Owning a business, and running a business, is a grand adventure. Every day a businessperson faces new challenges, new opportunities, and new kinds of excitement. Many businesspeople will say there's nothing more exciting than making customers happy by selling them products they love. Think of how happy you feel when you buy a new toy, or comic book, or shirt. Businesspeople, in your country and in other countries, make that possible for you.

If you're ready to learn more about business, go ahead and turn to the next chapter and let the adventure begin!

$$

CHAPTER 2
Being a Business Owner

So, do you think you might want to start your own business one day? Not everyone is meant to be a business owner, but more people would start businesses if they knew about the benefits of business ownership.

In the last chapter we discussed business owners and stockholders. There's another word that's used for someone who starts and runs a business. You may have even heard the word: *entrepreneur.* Below are a few questions designed to help you figure out whether or not you might make a good entrepreneur.

Are You Creative?

Artists, writers, singers, and actors are creative, but many of the best ideas in the world have come from entrepreneurs. An entrepreneur invented the automobile. Another entrepreneur came up with the best way to manufacture them. It was an entrepreneur who invented and marketed flat-screen TVs, video games, and smart phones. Sure it was a writer—J.K Rowling—who wrote *Harry Potter*, but it was an entrepreneur who started the publishing company that made the book available to readers around the world.

If you're creative, you have at least one trait many entrepreneurs share. By the way, you can be a writer, dancer, actor, singer, or artist and still be an entrepreneur. Lots of entrepreneurs had other jobs and other roles before they became entrepreneurs. Some professional athletes even become entrepreneurs after they quit playing professionally.

Some Artistic Entrepreneurs

Surely you know about Disney, the corporation that creates movies, books, games, and amusement parks that kids of all ages love. Did you know that the Walt Disney Company began with one man and a dream? Walt Disney started out as a cartoonist with a single cartoon, *Alice's Wonderland*, about a little girl in a cartoon world. Walt was clearly a gifted cartoonist. He could have made a good living working for someone else, creating cartoons for an animation company. Instead Walt decided to start his own company. Walt's brother joined him early on and eventually he hired other talented people. Under Walt's leadership, and inspired by his vision, those talented people built one of the most beloved companies in modern history.

There have been many other artistic people who've found success as entrepreneurs. Paul Newman was a famous actor who starred in many classic movies. In the 1980s he teamed up with a writer, A.E. Hotchner, to create a food company called "Newman's Own." The company, which

> ## Some Artistic Entrepreneurs (contd)
>
> sells packaged foods, such as healthy cookies, salad dressing, and spaghetti sauce, has been very successful. Gwen Stefani of the 90s pop band No Doubt is another great example. She started her own fashion clothing line in her kitchen. Since its start in 2004 her company, L.A.M.B., has grown into a worldwide business.

Are You a Good Problem Solver?

Any time you start a new business, problems are bound to show up. Some businesses find out they suddenly need more money. Some businesses learn that their product doesn't exactly work the way it's supposed to. Some businesses discover that they have workers who don't know how to do their jobs. Some businesses even face the problem of gaining too many customers too quickly.

While you can find some advice—from people, from books, and from articles—to help solve problems, many problems are very complex. Most problems don't have one clear right answer. That means that sometimes the business owner, the entrepreneur, must make very tough decisions. The better you are at problem solving, the more successful you and your business will be.

Do You See the Glass as Being Half-Full?

Another way of asking this question is, do you see opportunities where other people see roadblocks. Most successful entrepreneurs are always on the lookout for new opportunities, new possibilities. In fact, they tend to see the world that way: as a big buffet of possibilities.

Are You a Risk Taker?

There are bad risks and good risks. Jumping off the roof of your house onto the seat of your bicycle is a bad risk. How can you tell it's a bad risk? Well, there's a good chance you would end up getting hurt, so the downside is pretty big. And the upside? Actually, it's hard to see any upside from jumping off the roof onto the seat of your bicycle (aside from being able to brag to your friends for a couple of days, but that's not much upside).

A good risk is one that has a good chance a bringing a good result. Setting up a stand selling lemonade on a hot day is a pretty good risk. There's a good chance you would make money that day. But setting up a snow cone stand on a cold, snowy day might not be such a good risk.

Some people don't ever like to take any risks. It's fine that some people are built that way; it takes all kinds of people to make life on Planet Earth happen. But people who are never willing to take risks wouldn't make good entrepreneurs. People who only take bad risks wouldn't be good entrepreneurs either. A good entrepreneur can see opportunities and is willing to act on good ideas even though there may be some risk involved.

Are You Action-Oriented?

When you get a new idea, what do you do with it? Do you just keep thinking about it? Do you talk about it? Do you write it on a piece of paper and put that paper it in a shoebox in the bottom of your closet? Or do you do something with your idea? Do you try to make your idea happen?

Entrepreneurs tend to be people of action. They don't just sit around waiting for a lucky break. They don't just talk about their ideas, or brag about their big plans. They actually *do* something with their ideas.

That doesn't mean you should try to do something with all of your ideas. Some ideas are better than others. Some ideas are too risky. Some are just daydreams (and there's nothing wrong with a nice daydream now and then). But if you take action most times you have a good idea, then you share something in common with successful entrepreneurs.

Are You Responsible?

Probably a better question is, are you a hard worker? At your age you may not know for sure if you would be considered a hard worker or not. However, you do likely have an idea about whether you're responsible or not.

Do you finish all, or least most, of your homework? Do you turn it in on time? Do you do the chores your parents or caretakers ask you to do? When you do your homework and your chores, do you give it your very best effort? If you do all of these things, at least most of the time, then you're a pretty responsible person. You're also what most people would consider a hard worker.

Most entrepreneurs are very hard workers. When they are starting their businesses, they may spend most of their days working. They care a lot about their customers and their products, so working a lot isn't a problem for them. If you're someone who hates hard work then you might want to try becoming more responsible before you consider starting your own business. If you don't mind hard work, then you could succeed as an entrepreneur.

Are You a Good Communicator?

Good communication skills help with most jobs, and you'll have a much easier time as an entrepreneur if you know how to communicate with others. Are you good at talking to people? Are you good at persuading them? Entrepreneurs have to sell their ideas, so it's very important that they be able to persuade others.

Listening is a skill that's just as valuable as the skill of speaking. You may not have ever thought of listening as a skill, but it's actually a very important one. Business owners have to listen to their customers so they can make their products and their service better. Managers have to listen to their employees so they can make sure their employees are happy and are doing their jobs well. Listening is different than hearing. Hearing happens when you're not wearing ear buds and sound waves are able to reach your eardrums. Listening happens when you're focused on what another person is saying, and you're doing your best to understand that person. Can you think of times you were hearing someone when you really should have been listening?

Are You Determined?

What happens when you try something and it doesn't work right away? Do you give up easily, or do you keep trying until you make it work? Entrepreneurs are determined individuals. They know they're going to face hurdles, so they don't give up when difficulties come along. They keep trying until their idea works, or they change their approach. Milton Hershey failed in his first two attempts to launch a candy company. Fortunately he succeeded on his third try, and the world became a much sweeter place thanks to Hershey's chocolate.

What is a Market . . . And What Makes a Market Competitive?

Markets bring together buyers and sellers. Markets can be defined in a broad way, or in a very narrow way. For example, you can talk about the market for entertainment. That would include a lot of things, such as movie theaters, professional sporting events, video games, graphic novels, etc. If we focused on the market for movies we'd have a narrower market than the market for entertainment in general. We could tighten our focus even further and discuss the market for first-run movies at movie theaters, which would be different than movies viewed on Netflix or rented through Redbox.

Markets can also be defined by where they're located. The market for first-run movies at movie theaters on the West Coast is a little different than the market for first-run movies at movie theaters in the Midwest. If you don't believe they're different, go online and compare the ticket prices in Lincoln, Nebraska to the ticket prices in Los Angeles, California!

Some markets are more *competitive* than others. When a market is competitive it simply means that there are lots of sellers offering customers the same, or a similar, product. The market for pizza is pretty competitive in most

What is a Market . . . And What Makes a Market Competitive? (contd)

cities because there are lots of pizza restaurants trying to sell their pies. The pizza at Mama Mia's Pizzeria may not be exactly the same as the pizza at Bob's Pizza Shack, but it's fairly similar.

Other markets are less competitive, like the market for cell phones. There aren't a whole lot of companies that produce cell phones. Another example is electricity. In most cities and towns, if you want to buy electricity you have only one choice: the local electric company. When there is a market with only one seller—such as the market for electricity—that company is said to have a *monopoly.*

Of course, some business ideas are never going to work out. Maybe they involve the wrong products, or the right products offered at the wrong time or offered to the wrong people. Some businesses are bound to fail—that's just the nature of a competitive market. But some people give up much too easily. Those people don't usually make the best entrepreneurs.

So, how did you answer the questions? Are you a creative, action-oriented risk taker who also happens to be a good problem solver? Are you a determined and responsible person? Are you a good communicator, meaning that you know how to talk to people *and* how to listen to them? If you're all, or even most, of these things then you share some basic traits with all the greatest entrepreneurs who ever lived. You could become a great entrepreneur one day yourself. But in order to make that happen you're going to need a solid business idea.

Maybe you already have an idea for a business you'd like to start. If you do, that's wonderful! But if you're not sure what kind of business you want to start, that's okay, too. The next chapter will offer you some "idea starters" to help get your creative juices flowing!

$$

CHAPTER 3
Finding a Business Idea

Some people think that all the good ideas in the world have been used up. That's not true, and it will never be true. There will always be new ideas. Lots of new things are invented every year. Lots of businesses are created every year, and many of them are based on new ideas.

So how do you come up with an idea for a business?

Business ideas can come from anyplace. You may already have a good idea for a new business, but don't worry if you don't yet. This chapter contains several business idea starters, all designed to help you generate great concepts for new businesses.

Idea Starter #1: Solve a problem

One of the best ways to come up with a good business idea is to think of a problem that needs to be solved. So many great inventions and businesses came into being because they solved problems for people. The automobile solved a problem for people, but autos were so expensive in the early years that only very wealthy individuals could afford them. Henry Ford saw a way to solve *that* problem. Ford invented the assembly line, which allowed cars to be produced at a much lower cost. Of course, most other manufacturers also began producing their goods using the assembly line, so Ford's idea—a true innovation—solved lots of problems for lots of people.   Y o u can probably think of many other products that came about because they solved problems for people. Pens with erasable ink. Doggy daycares. Portable power banks (used for charging cell phones and other devices without an electrical outlet). How many examples can you think of?

What is an Innovation?

Some people think an innovation is the same as a new invention. While it's true that inventions are usually innovations, an innovation doesn't have to involve an invention or a new technology. A new way of doing things can also be thought of as an innovation. For example, Henry Ford didn't invent the automobile, but he did come up with a new way to make them. The assembly line was an innovation that changed the way nearly all things are manufactured. Sam Walton didn't invent the concept of a retail store, but he developed many innovations in the world of retailing, which made his company, Wal-Mart, the most successful retailer in the world. Not all innovators are famous. Melitta Benz, a German housewife, came up with the technique for brewing filtered coffee, which is the way most coffee is still made today. Innovators like Henry Ford, Sam Walton, Melitta Benz, and Steve Jobs are people who shake up the system and change the way things are done. Can you think of some innovators or some innovations that have changed life for the better?

Idea Starter #2 Borrow an idea you've seen someplace else

There are plenty of businesses that started because some-one saw an idea one place and brought it to another. One example is the American car sharing company Zipcar. A cus-tomer of Zipcar doesn't own a car herself; she pays a fee to use the car only when she needs it. Zipcar has been a very successful company, but the idea didn't start in America. The businesspeople who started the company saw the idea first in Europe.

A lot of businesses begin in one state, like California or New York, and then spread to other states. Sometimes the businesses spread through something called franchising. Sometimes other businesspeople visiting from other states borrow the ideas and take them home to their own states. Maybe on your next vacation you might see a business you've never seen before. Ask yourself if it's something that might work where you live.

What is Franchising?

Franchising is a setup where a company gives a person per-mission to use the company's business concept, its products, its name, its logo, etc. The person has to pay the company for the right to use those things. In exchange, the person buying the franchise gets help from the company in setting up his business.

Why would a person want to buy a franchise? A fran-chise is sort of a like a "business in a box." The company

What is Franchising? (contd)

has proven that its concept works, that people like its products. Sometimes the company is very well-known across the nation, or even around the world. McDonald's is an example of a company that sells franchises. If you've eaten at a McDonald's restaurant, there's a good chance you've eaten at a store that was a franchise, owned by a local person who bought the rights to sell McDonald's food from the McDonald's Corporation. If that same person had started his own hamburger restaurant from scratch, what are the chances it would become as well-known as McDonald's? Not very high. After all, is there anything in the world more recognizable than the golden arches?

The downsides of buying a franchise include the fact that it may cost a lot of money upfront. Most people who buy franchises are also required to make regular payments to the company for as long as the franchise is in operation. In addition, people who buy franchises give up a lot of control over how business is done. They have to agree to run the business the way the company wants it operated. A person who wants to control her own business and try out her own ideas would be better off staying away from franchising and starting her own business from scratch.

Borrowing vs. Stealing

If you borrow someone else's business idea, you have to make sure that you really are borrowing and not stealing. In many cases it's okay to borrow an idea. Suppose that while visiting your cousin in a neighboring town you saw someone selling chili dogs outside the fields where little league baseball games and soccer games are played. Let's assume, for this example, that the vendor calls his business Chuck's Chili Dogs and that he uses a cool logo featuring an image of a dachshund and a chili pepper. You could borrow the basic idea—i.e., you could go back to your home town and sell chili dogs at the little league fields. But it wouldn't be a good idea to call your business Chuck's Chili Dogs. It also wouldn't be a good idea to use Chuck's logo. If you used Chuck's name and logo, most people would consider that stealing. In fact, if Chuck has his name and logo trademarked, or legally protected, he can sue you in court!

Idea Starter #3: Turn something you already do into a business

If you already have something you love to do, and something you're already good at, why not figure out a way to turn it into a business? For example, suppose that you enjoy making jewelry and that you're good at it. You could potentially create a business selling your handmade jewelry. If you have passion for jewelry making, you'll only get better and better at creating designs people love. Of course, you'll likely face a lot of competition, but if you really enjoy doing it you just may come up a million-dollar design.

It always helps if you love what you do, but is it okay if you just *like* what you do? Suppose you're really good at yard work: mowing, trimming, weeding, etc. You're so good at it, people compliment your work after you've finished a lawn. Maybe you don't *love* to do yard work the way you love to play videogames or paint with watercolors, but you don't mind doing the work. What you *do* enjoy is the feeling you get from a job well done. You appreciate all the pats on the back people give you when they look at a lawn you've cut and trimmed. And you certainly appreciate the money you earn for doing such work (including the tips you receive because you're so good at it). Could you possibly create a yard work business? Absolutely. It doesn't have to be your dream job—i.e., the job you want to do for the rest of your life. If you're good at something, and if you like doing it well enough, you could turn it into a profitable business.

Idea Starter #4: Create a business using stuff that's already around

This one is similar to turning something you already do into a business. The difference is that instead of focusing on things you already do, you're using resources you already have available. For example, if you had an ice cream-making machine sitting in your basement, it would make sense to at least consider starting an ice cream business.

You probably don't have an ice cream machine in your basement—at least not one big enough to make gallons and gallons of ice cream every day. But you surely have other things, other resources, around you that can use. Is there a rake in your garage? You can start a leaf raking business. Do you own the latest, greatest animation software? Think of all the businesses in your town that would love to have their own animated video promoting their products.

Idea Starter #5: Figure out a way to make people's lives easier, better, or more fun

One young man had an idea for a business that was easy to start. Because of daylight savings time, most people have to reset their clocks twice each year. It can take a while to reset all the clocks in an average-sized house. A lot of people lead busy lives and they'd rather not waste of time resetting all those clocks. The young man in this story went door-to-door offering to reset all the clocks in a house for a fee. He may not make millions of dollars resetting clocks twice per year, but he can make some extra spending money. Over time he could even save up his earnings and start a bigger business.

Amazon became a huge company by making people's lives easier. With Amazon, a customer can order a product and have it shipped to her house in just a couple of days. Could shopping get any easier than that? Believe it or not there was a time when families—mostly the women of the family—had to wash clothes by hand. Think of how much easier life became when the washing machine was invented.

What about businesses that make life better or more fun for people? Movie theaters, amusement parks, companies that sell CDs and music downloads, magazine publishers, ice cream stands, and massage spas are all good examples.

If you can think of a way to make people's lives easier, better, or more fun, you may have a great business idea on your hands.

Idea Starter #6: Fulfill a need in the market

An untold number of businesses were started because someone saw a hole that needed to be filled. Imagine that you moved to a town and noticed that it had no car wash. If there are enough people in the town—and enough cars that need to be washed—it could make very good sense to open up a car wash in the town. The same could be true for many other types of businesses. Bakeries. Daycare centers. Coffee shops.

When you look around, do you see any unmet needs? Do you live in a town without a delivery service? Maybe there are no singing telegram companies or DJ companies where you live. Maybe there several bakeries, but none that serve gluten-free bread or pastries. Maybe there's a good coffee shop in town, but it's always so crowded that people end up leaving because they don't wish to wait in line. Each of these scenarios involves a gap or a hole in the market just waiting to be filled.

Take a careful look around. Notice the businesses that are there . . . and then notice what's not there that really *should* be.

Of course, many new business ideas may fall into more than one of these idea starter categories. You may think of a business concept that fills a hole in the market while also making people's lives easier. Or you may come up with an idea that solves a problem and happens to be something you already do well. Actually it's not a bad thing at all if your idea falls into more than one of the idea starter categories.

Let's suppose that you take a look around and notice that your town has a pet daycare, but you talk to some cat owners who don't like to use the pet daycare. The cat own-ers tell you that their cats get stressed out when they're taken away from their home environment. Also, there are a lot of barking dogs at the pet daycare, and that's a stressful environment for any cat. You happen to love animals, espe-cially cats. Some of the cat owners you know travel for long stretches of time, and they don't have relatives nearby who can care for their cats while they're away. That's a real prob-lem for those cat owners.

It occurs to you that you could possibly start up a business caring for people's cats while they're away. Your service—as you see it unfolding in your mind's eye—would involve you traveling to the cat owner's house, feeding the cat, refilling its water, cleaning up any messes, and perhaps giving the cat some attention. If the cat owner is away on a trip, you could also bring in the mail, pick up any packages that are sitting on the front step, bring in the trash cans, and other similar small jobs. It's a business idea that fills an unmet need in the market since the local pet daycare doesn't provide home service. Your busi-ness concept also solves a problem for people, namely cat own-ers—and possibly other pet owners—who travel. Additionally, the concept involves something you already love to do—i.e., care for animals.

This business concept could be a real winner, but before launching it you'll want to do some more research. You'll also want to make a plan for how you're going to reach your busi-ness goals. In later chapters we'll discuss the kinds of research entrepreneurs typically do before launching a new business venture. We'll also cover the basics of business plans. In cover-ing these topics, and other topics, we'll come back to the home pet care business concept. We'll use it an example throughout the rest of this book.

Instead of referring to it repeatedly as the "home pet care business concept," we'll work on coming up with a shorter, catchier name for the business. In fact, coming up with business names is the whole focus of the next chapter.

$$

CHAPTER 4
Naming Your Business

After you've settled on an idea for a business, you'll want to start thinking of a name for it. Of course, there's no rule that says you have to name your business right away, but it can be helpful to do it early. Naming something makes it feel more real.

Can you remember the last time there was a new baby in your family? Most likely the parents started thinking of names long before the baby was born. They might have even started calling the baby by some name. Naming a baby, even before it's born, makes the baby feel like a real part of the family. Similarly, naming your business before it's born makes it feel like a real living thing.

There are other similarities between naming a baby and naming a business. People sometimes form opinions about other people based on their name. For example, if someone has a unique name—such as Lady Gaga—it's natural to assume that the person also has a unique personality. If a person's name sounds unfamiliar or very different from the names we're used to hearing, we're likely to assume that the person is from another country or culture. In addition, a name that is hard to pronounce or spell may take longer to learn and remember.

Although there are some similarities between naming a baby and naming a business, there are also big differences. First of all, there are lots a great baby naming books on the market. Many of these books include lists of names for boys and for girls, along with meanings for the suggested names. You can't really find books featuring lists of business names (although there are random name generators available on the Internet).

Another way naming babies is different from naming businesses is that, with babies, repeats are allowed. You can have millions of Johns and Marys and Mohammeds, but you can't have millions of Microsofts. You can't even have *two* Microsofts. If you started a computer company and tried to name it Microsoft, the company called Microsoft that has been around for decades would sue you into oblivion. Actually they would probably first send you a letter asking you to stop using their name, and then if you ignored their request they would sue you into oblivion. However it happened, the company would make you stop using its name because Bill Gates—or someone involved with Microsoft in the company's early days—thought of it first. Microsoft has in fact trademarked the name *Microsoft* so that no one else can use it.

Naming businesses is different from naming babies in another important way. Although people sometimes make assumptions about us based on our name, the fact is we were given our name either before we were born or shortly thereafter. Our parents didn't wait to get to know us and our personality for a few weeks or months before naming us. They just picked a name they liked and wrote it down on a legal form.

When you name a business you know something about its personality. You don't know what it may end up becoming one day, but you know what you intend it to be. For example, if you're starting a business that sells healthy smoothies, you have a pretty good idea the business won't be selling tobacco products—or other unhealthy items—ten years down the road. The company is focused on health, so you may want a name that conjures a healthy image in people's minds. In other words, you want to consider choosing a name that tells people something about your products and your company.

On the other hand, you also want to avoid being too specific or narrow in selecting a business name. Why is that so? Just imagine that you have a great recipe for a delicious healthy blueberry smoothie. People ask for you to make your smoothie so often that you decide to build a business around it. Because you only have one recipe—only one type of smoothie—you decide to name your business something like *The Blueberry Smoothie Shack*. Can you see why that name might eventually be a problem? Soon after you open your business, you'll likely discover that people want other flavors of smoothies as well. Someone looking for a banana-flavored smoothie may pass up your store. Even if you start to offer other flavors in addition to blueberry, your name suggests that your product is limited.

The Smoothie Shack would be a better name than *The Blueberry Smoothie Shack* because it offers you room to expand your product offerings. Of course, it's possible that one day you might want to offer other healthy refreshments in addition to smoothies. If those other products became a large part of your business, then the name *The Smoothie Shack* might no longer be a good fit. You may want to brainstorm and look for a name that creates an image of health without limiting you to just selling smoothies.

While Ur Away: What's In a Name?

Okay, so it's time to sit down and come up with a name for the home pet care service business concept we discussed in the last chapter. Since we're assuming that the idea came out of the complaints of cat owners, we could choose a name that involves felines. The problem with that approach is fairly obvious. We may want to also offer services to fish owners, bird owners, hamster owners, iguana owners, and dog owners whose dogs don't like the doggy daycare. For that reason, we may want to stick with a more general term and keep the word "cat" out of the name. In choosing a name we may also want to highlight the fact that our service involves visits to the customer's home. That, after all, is an important part of the business concept.

Let's suppose that after a great deal of brainstorming, we settle on the name *While Ur Away Home Pet Care*. Note that we considered other names, but discovered they were already being used by similar businesses in other cities, such as *The Pet Patrol, On the Go Pet Care, and Pet Care 2 You*. It's not always a good idea to use misspellings in a business name ("Ur" instead of "You're"), but it may make sense for this concept. Thanks to texting, nearly everyone knows that "ur" is shorthand for "you're" or "your." Using the shorthand in this case gives the business name a young, slightly trendy vibe. Also, *While Ur Away* will appear more streamlined on

While Ur Away: What's In a Name? (contd)

a flyer or webpage than *While You're Away*. The name may not fully get across the idea that it's a mobile pet sitting service, but it does at least hint at that notion. A good slogan or logo can help shore up the mobile aspect of the business so that customers understand very clearly what the service is.

We'll discuss slogans and logos in more depth in a later chapter. For now, we've got a name we can use for the sample business. A business name can always be changed later in the planning process, but having a name early on goes a long way in making the business feel more real.

After you've brainstormed and come up with a name that fits your business perfectly, you'll want to do some research. First of all, do an Internet search and make sure no other company similar to yours is using the name. A quick Internet search is only a starting place. To make sure the name is truly available, you'll need to do a trademark search. Many states also have websites where you can register a business name and check to see if anyone else in your state is already using a given name.

Hopefully the name you chose for your business is available. If not, then you'll need to brainstorm some more. If it is available, that's great, but it doesn't mean your research is done. You'll want to make sure you can find a suitable URL, or domain name, for your business. In this day and age nearly every business has a website, and you'll want a domain name for your website that's somehow related to your business name or concept.

What is a URL and how do you get one?

URL stands for "uniform resource locator." You don't have to remember that phrase. Most people simply refer to it as a website address or a domain name. For example, www. nps.gov is the URL for the National Park Service. The URL for the American Red Cross is www.redcross.org. Can you guess the URL for the National Football League? That's right—it's www.nfl.com.

It's not too difficult to get a URL for your business website. To get one you'll need to visit what's called a domain name registrar, which is a company that registers URLs or domain names. There are several companies that offer this service. GoDaddy.com, Name.com, and DreamHost.com are good examples. You can always do an Internet search on "Registering a domain name," and you'll find lots of options for securing a URL for your business.

If the name you chose is available, and a good URL is available, you could go ahead and name the business. However, before proceeding, it would be a good idea for you to do a little more research. Have you asked other people what they think of the name? What if people find your business name to be awkward or confusing? What if they have a hard time pronouncing the name or spelling it? What if it looks funny printed on a page?

Type the name, in different fonts and colors, and see how it looks on a page. Imagine what it would look like in giant letters on a sign. Ask others to look at it printed on a page and to give you their opinion. Tell people your business name and ask them what kinds of images it stirs up in their minds. You might be surprised by the feedback people give you.

Once you've completed all of your research and you've found an available name that people understand, that looks great on a printed page (and a webpage), that rolls off the tongue like Cheerios, you're ready to start thinking about a mission statement for your business. The next chapter will help you set goals and create a mission statement that will guide your company toward success.

$$

CHAPTER 5
Setting Goals and Creating a Mission

Y ou've probably set goals for yourself sometime in the past. Maybe you set a goal to get a certain grade in a certain subject. If you play a sport you might have set a goal to score a certain number of goals or touchdowns or homeruns during the season. You may have a goal for your future career. Maybe you'd like to go to college one day and study graphic design or computer programming. Maybe you'd like to act in a Broadway play or work as a movie director. Perhaps you're focused on getting a job as soon as you're old enough and saving up enough money to buy your own car. Those would all be worthy personal goals.

Businesses also set goals. Most businesses set goals for how much they'd like to grow in a given time period. For example, the managers of XYZ Company might decide that they'd like the company to double its sales over the next five years. Another company, ABC Corp., may set a goal of cutting its expenses by twenty percent over the next year.

What Are Expenses?

You've probably heard the term *expenses* before, but you may be foggy about what it means. That's understandable. If you've never worked in a business or studied business concepts, some of the jargon might seem a bit foreign.

Expenses are items a business must pay for on a regular basis. Businesses that hire workers must pay those workers' wages. Wages are a type of expense. Many businesses use raw materials to create a product. For example, a company that produces wooden baseball bats—Barb's Bat Factory—will need to buy lots of wood. When Barb's Bat Factory pays for the wood, it's paying an expense. The company will also have to pay the electric and water bills—those are expenses, too. If Barb's Bats Factory advertises its baseball bats, it will pay advertising expense.

Households also have expenses, such as rent, food, utilities, tuition, etc. Most businesses have a lot more expenses than a typical household. But just as it is for a household, a business would rather have lower expenses than higher expenses.

Good goals are well-defined and can easily be measured. Saying that you'd like to become better at math isn't the best goal. Actually it's a good goal to strive for, but it could be stated differently. How can you measure that you're getting better at math? Think of a way to measure it and add that to your goal. For instance, you could say that you want to raise your grade from a B to an A—that's a well-defined, measurable goal.

What would make the goal even better would be to add a time-frame. "I would like to raise my math grade from a B to an A over the next three months." That's a *very* solid goal.

When you start a new business you'll want to set some goals for the business. Define the goals well, and make sure you come up with a way to measure them. It's not too difficult to measure business goals, since most of them are expressed in terms of dollars and cents. Also consider adding a timeframe to your business goals. "My business will earn $2,000 during its first year" is an example of a good measurable business goal.

From Goals to Mission

You've probably heard the word *mission* as it relates to military operations, or situations involving a battle or struggle. The word shows up a lot in certain kinds of movies and video games. But missions aren't just for Navy Seals and Jedi knights. Businesses also have missions, which are expressed in written form in their mission statements.

A **mission statement** is a written explanation of a company's philosophy. It's basically a philosophy of doing business. Goals can be part of a mission statement, but many mission statements include something more. Many companies like to include something about its values or guiding beliefs in its mission statement.

A great example is the mission statement Steve Jobs created for Apple early on. Apple's mission was "to make a contribution to the world by making tools for the mind that advance humankind." Even though Apple's official mission statement has changed since the company's early days, anyone can see that Apple is still carrying out the mission Steve Jobs created for the company decades ago. Jobs set out to advance humankind by making "tools for the mind"; Apple has done exactly that, perhaps better than almost any other company that exists. Note that when goals are included as part of a mission statement, they're generally not expressed in a measurable way. That's not a problem for a mission statement. A company's mission statement offers general guidance. Most companies will have separate written goals that are more specific in nature.

Another great example of a mission statement that includes a firm's guiding beliefs is the one the founders of Ben & Jerry's created for their ice cream company. Their mission statement says a lot in one sentence: "To make, distribute and sell the finest quality of all natural ice cream and euphoric concoctions with a continued commitment to incorporating wholesome, natural ingredients and promoting business practices that respect the Earth and the Environment."

There are a lot of big words in that mission statement, but it essentially says that the company is going to sell good-tasting ice cream with healthy, natural ingredients and it will do so in an environmentally friendly way. The mission statement defines what the company is and describes how the company will do business. A mission statement doesn't have to be as long or include as many big words as Ben & Jerry's. Wal-Mart's mission statement "To help people save money so they can live better," is very simple and to-the-point. Search the Internet for examples of other mission statements. Think of the companies you like, or of the companies whose products you use. Find out what their mission statements are. It's not a good idea to copy another company's mission statement, but you can get some good ideas that will inspire you when you write your own.

When you create a mission statement you're in effect making a written statement of what your company is and why it exists. Must you absolutely have a written mission statement on paper before you launch your company? No, you could launch a company and maybe even build it up to a decent size without having a mission statement in place. But a mission statement isn't just something that you create for yourself as the business owner. A company's mission statement is intended for everyone who is affected by the company. Those people are often referred to as **stakeholders**.

Stockholders vs. Stakeholders

Stockholders, as mentioned in a previous chapter, are individuals who own shares of stock in a corporation. They are the owners of a corporation. The **stakeholders** of a company include the company's stockholders, or owners, among others. Customers are stakeholders. A company's workers, or employees, are stakeholders. Other companies that sell supplies to a company are among its stakeholders. The people who live in the community where a company is located can also be considered stakeholders.

When a company is new it doesn't usually have many stakeholders. As a company grows, it affects more and more people. A large company like Google has millions of stakeholders (you might even be one of them!). Imagine that a company you start could one day have hundreds, or thousands, or even millions of stakeholders scattered all over the world!

While Ur Away: Setting Down Goals and "Missioning" Up

We need a mission statement and some solid goals for our sample business, *While Ur Away Home Pet Care*. Let's suppose that after studying the mission statements of several other companies, and after searching your heart deeply, you settle on the following mission statement:

Our mission is to treat your pets with the best care possible—the care they deserve—so you don't have to worry while you're away from home.

At the outset you also set the following one-year goals:

1. By the end of Year 1, the company will have revenues of at least $5,000.
2. By the end of Year 1, the company will have profits of at least $4,000.
3. By the end of Year 1, the company will have a plan in place to reach at least 20,000 potential customers through our advertising efforts.

This mission statement and some of the goals also appear in the sample business plan at the end of the book.

It's worth spending some time to come up with a good strong mission statement. Start out by asking yourself why your business exists—or why it's going to exist. What will it do that makes it stand out from other businesses? Can you write a mission statement that inspires your employees (when you have some) to do a better job? Will your mission statement make your customers proud that they do business with you? More importantly, when you read your company's mission statement, is it something you deeply believe? If so, then you have a mission statement that will help guide your newly created company to success.

$$

CHAPTER 6
Making a Plan

Whenever your family goes on vacation, it's likely the case that someone makes a plan. Maybe your whole family sits around a table and helps with the plan. As everyone knows, there are lots of decisions to make with any vacation plan. Should we go to Florida or Washington D.C.? Should we go to Disneyworld first or should we go to the beach first? What should we take with us on the trip? Are we allowed to take friends along?

It's always possible that a vacation won't go exactly as planned. Maybe a hurricane blows in on the day you were planning to visit the beach. Maybe while driving to the alligator aquarium you come across a better opportunity (an alpaca petting zoo!). Maybe while on vacation you save someone's prize poodle from drowning and you receive a million-dollar reward. Imagine all the new vacation possibilities you'd have open to you with a million newfound dollars in your pocket!

When you make a vacation plan you don't have to be totally married to it. Things can change if they need to, or if you just want them to. A business plan is like that, too. A business plan lays out a company's goals and explains how the company will reach those goals. Usually a business plan also gives some information about the people who will work to move the company toward its goals. The business plan explains the company's product or products in detail, and it also explains how the product will be marketed.

Marketing will be discussed in a later chapter. Many of the other parts of a business plan will also be discussed in later chapters. For now, we'll take a general look at the main parts of a business plan.

Main Parts of a Typical Business Plan

Company Overview – A general description of the company, its product or products, and its mission statement.

Organization and Team – Who are the members of your team? Why are your team members a good fit for your business? What skills or experience do your team members have that will help your business? Who will be in charge of what in your company?

Products/Services – A more in-depth description of the company's products and/or services. What's different or special about your company's products or services? What are the main benefits customers get when they use your products or services?

Business Environment – Also sometimes known as the Competitive Environment or Market Analysis, this section discusses the industry your company is in. Who are your main competitors? How many people, or other businesses, are out there who might be your customers one day?

Marketing Plan – How will you get the word out about your company and its product(s)?

Company Strategy – How do you plan to reach your business goals? Other details may be included in this section. For example, how many locations will you have? What hours will you be open for business? Where will you get your supplies? Sometimes this section is known as the Operation Plan.

Financial Plan – How much will it cost to launch your business? How much do you expect to make in the near future? How much do you expect to make a little farther into the future?

There's not one correct way to write a business plan. Some business plans have more sections than those listed above. Some business plans are a few pages long, while others may be dozens of pages in length. The important thing is that your plan covers the main points, and that it helps keep you on track toward reaching your goals. It's true that not all businesses create a business plan before launching. Usually you'll need one if you're trying to borrow money from a bank, or if you're trying to attract investors.

What Is An Investor?

An *investor* is a person who uses his money to attempt to make more money. People invest money in stocks, bonds, real estate, gold, fine art, and many other things. When an investor puts his money into something it's known as an *investment*.

What Is An Investor? (contd)

For each of his investments, the investor hopes to earn a return, meaning that he'll get more money out of the investment than the amount he put into it. For example, suppose an investor—we'll call him Mr. Green—invests $10,000 in the stock of Acme Corporation. If a year after buying the Acme stock, Mr. Green is able to sell it for $11,000, then he would earn a return of $1,000, or 10 percent (1,000/10,000 = 10 percent).

Some investors like to invest in startup companies. When an investor invests in a startup company, he typically becomes part owner of the company. Many investors will ask to see a company's business plan before they agree to invest money in the business.

At the end of this book you'll find a sample business plan for our sample business, *While Ur Away Home Pet Care*. Consider using it as a model for developing your own plan for your own business concept. There are also many websites that feature sample business plans for a wide variety of industries. It's not a good idea to copy another plan word for word, but you can certainly use an existing business plan as a guide.

$$

CHAPTER 7
Sizing Up Your Business

L ots of people confuse marketing with advertising—they see the two as one in the same. Advertising is part of marketing but there's much more to marketing than just getting the word out about your product. Marketing also involves figuring out who your customers are, what their needs are, and how to best meet their needs with your product. We'll discuss advertising and promotions in a later chapter. For now, we'll focus on the research aspect of marketing, beginning with some tools you can use to identify your customers and learn some basic information about them.

Identifying Your Customers

How can you figure out who your customers are? Before you spend a lot of time and money launching a business, it would be good to know that people are actually interested in your product. Most companies engage in some form of market research. Companies can use market research to find out how many consumers might be interested in their products, how much those consumers would be willing to pay for the product, and the best ways to advertise to those consumers. Surveys and focus groups are two common tools companies use to research potential markets.

Surveys

A survey is a list of questions people are asked to answer. The questions aren't random—they're specially designed. When you design a survey, a lot of thought should go into the questions. You want to make sure the answers to the questions give you useful information. What makes a question a good survey question? Perhaps one way to learn about writing good survey questions is to take a look at some questions that would not be so useful in a survey.

Bad Survey Question–Example #1:

Rock jewelry is really cool stuff. You would definitely buy some, wouldn't you?

This question is what's known as a leading question. If you want to find out someone's honest opinion about something, you shouldn't include statements that may sway their answer. Keep the wording of the question as neutral as possible.

Bad Survey Question–Example #2:

Would you pay more than $5 for a bracelet made of polished stones?

This question isn't totally terrible, but it could be better. What if most people answer "yes," meaning that they would be willing to pay more than $5 for a bracelet made of polished stones? The problem is you'd have no idea how much more than $5 they'd be willing to pay. Some of them might be willing to pay $20 and others might only be willing to pay $5.50. It would be better to give people a range of possible answers, covering many different potential price levels for the product.

Bad Survey Question–Example #3:

On average, how many bracelets do you buy each year? (Circle one)

0 to 2 bracelets	*2 to 4 bracelets*
4 to 8 bracelets	*8 or more bracelets*

The question part of this question isn't bad, but there's a problem with the options offered for answers. The choices involve overlapping categories. What if a person filling out the survey buys 2 bracelets each year? Should the person circle the first category, 0 to 2 bracelets, or the second category, 2 to 4 bracelets? Fortunately this is a problem that's easily fixed. There would be no problem if the categories were 0 to 2 bracelets, 3 to 5 bracelets, 6 to 8 bracelets, and 9 or more bracelets.

Bad Survey Question–Example #4:

On average, how many bracelets do you buy each year? (Circle one)

1 to 3 bracelets	*4 to 6 bracelets*
7 to 9 bracelets	*10 or more bracelets*

This question is very similar to the one before it. Only the categories offered for answers are different. The categories don't overlap; that's not the problem here. The problem is that the categories don't include all the possible answers. What if the person filling out the survey doesn't buy any bracelets? There's no category the person can circle since the lowest range begins at 1. Again, this is an easy problem to correct. If the lowest category started at 0, there would be no problem at all.

Bad Survey Question–Example #5:

Do you like jewelry?

Maybe this is the kind of question you'd ask a new friend, just to begin learning something about that person. But it doesn't make a very good survey question. What if you asked 100 people this question and 94 of them answered yes. You would know that 94 percent of the people you surveyed like jewelry, but you wouldn't know anything else. What kinds of jewelry do they like? Do you they like it just a little bit or do they like it a lot? Do they actually like to buy jewelry, or do they just like it if it's given as a gift. If they buy jewelry, how much would they be willing to spend on a nice piece of jewelry? A question like this is too general and really just takes up precious space on a survey.

Bad Survey Question–Example #6:

Do you like bracelets and necklaces?

This question might seem like it's better than the previous one because it's a bit more specific. Unfortunately, it's still a bad question. If a person answers "yes," then you can safely assume that the person likes both types of jewelry. But what if a person answers "no"? Does that mean she doesn't like bracelets *and* she doesn't' like necklaces? What is she likes bracelets but hates necklaces? How should she answer the question? It would be better to break this question into two separate questions, one about bracelets and the other about necklaces. As we'll see later in this chapter, there may be a better way to ask people about the kinds of jewelry they like to purchase.

Bad Survey Question–Example #7:

What percentage of your yearly budget do you spend on jewelry purchases? (Circle one)

0 to 5%	6 to 11%	12 to 16%	17 to 22%
23 to 28%	29 to 34%	35 to 40%	41 to 46%
47 to 52%	53 to 58%	59 to 64%	65 to 70%
71 to 76%	77 to 82%	83 to 88%	89 to 94%
95 to 100%			

This question has two problems. First, there are way too many options, too many categories, offered as answers. It would be better to keep it down to five or six categories at most. The second problem with this question is that many people have a hard time thinking in terms of percentages. They might circle one of the categories, but their answer could just be a wild guess. If the people you ask to complete your survey are all math lovers, you might be fine asking about percentages. But surely some of the people interested in your jewelry won't be math whizzes.

Let's take a look at some questions that would be good for a survey. We'll stick with the jewelry example for now, and later we'll consider some examples for the sample business, *While Ur Away*.

1. How many pieces of jewelry do you buy each year on average? (Circle one)

   None   1 to 5   6 to 10   More than 10

2. What kinds of jewelry do you buy? (Check all that apply)
   ❑ Bracelets
   ❑ Necklaces
   ❑ Rings
   ❑ Earrings
   ❑ Other (please specify what kind):_____

3. Where do you buy jewelry? (Check all that apply)
   ❑ Jewelry stores
   ❑ Department stores (e.g., Macys, JC Pennys)
   ❑ Big box retailers (e.g., Wal-Mart, Target)
   ❑ Online
   ❑ Other (please specify where):_____

Together these questions could form the basis of a good survey for a market research study on jewelry. There should also be some questions about price. You'd want to know how much people are willing to pay, on average, for a product like yours. It's also common for market researchers to ask about things like age, gender, and household income. You'd probably like to know whether males or females are more interested in your product. You also might want to know if older people or younger people tend to favor your product.

It can be tricky asking about household income. If you're giving your survey to kids, some of them won't know their household income. Many people don't like to share this kind of information. Such people would likely leave a survey question like that blank. People are usually more willing to answer questions like those if the survey is anonymous, meaning that you don't ask them to identify themselves.

Analyzing the Results of Your Survey

Some of the tools companies use to analyze survey results are very complicated. You can still gain some useful information from survey results, even without using complex statistical techniques. For each question on your survey, you can calculate how participants responded on a percentage basis. Suppose for example that you asked 100 people the question "What kinds of jewelry do you buy?" (Yes, it's one of the sample questions from above.) Suppose further that 75 of the participants said they buy bracelets, 90 said they buy necklaces, 64 buy rings, 52 buy earrings, and 43 buy some other type of jewelry. To calculate a percentage for each question, you simply divide the number who checked the box by the total number of participants—which is 100

Analyzing the Results of Your Survey (contd)

in this example. So 75% buy bracelets, 90% buy necklaces, and so on. If you carefully picked the 100 people you gave surveys to, then you can reasonably assume that those percentages would apply to the general population—or to the population of people who are like the 100 individuals you asked to complete your survey.

If these were your actual results, you might decide to start out offering necklaces, since more people appear to buy necklaces than any other type of jewelry. You might decide that you don't want to offer earrings, or that you don't want to offer too many earrings, since a relatively small percentage of the participants buy earrings. It should be pointed out that these results are hypothetical, or imaginary. If you were to ask 100 people to answer the question about jewelry you'll likely get completely different results.

While Ur Away: Sizing Up the Home Pet Care Market

Here are some sample survey questions you might use to research the home pet care market in your area:

1. What kinds of pets do you own and how many of each?
   - ❏ Cats Number: ____
   - ❏ Dogs Number: ____
   - ❏ Birds Number: ____
   - ❏ Fish Number: ____

❏ Reptiles Number:_____
❏ Other Number:_____

2. On average, how many days per year do you travel?

Less than 3   4 to 10   11 to 19
20 to 30   More than 30

3. How do you provide care for your pet(s) when you
    travel? (Check all that apply)
    ❏ I take my pet(s) to a pet daycare
    ❏ I ask relatives, friends, or neighbors to help out
    ❏ I pay someone to come provide care for my pets
    ❏ I leave my pets on their own with plenty of food and
       water
    ❏ Not applicable (I don't have pets or I'm not away from
       home for long periods)

Focus Groups

Focus groups are another tool companies use to gather
information from consumers. Focus groups are different from
surveys in a couple of ways. Some surveys are given over the
phone and some are done face to face, but many are sent out
through the mail or through electronic means, such as email.
Focus groups are generally done in person. A survey is typically completed by one person at a time. Focus groups involve
several people providing information as a group. Also, the questions asked in a focus group session may be more open-ended
than the questions in a survey.

With a focus group study you gather several people into
a room with a person who leads the group. The leader, also

known as the facilitator, walks the group through a series of questions designed to gather information about a company or product. Oftentimes the sessions are video recorded so that company managers can study the session later.

In many focus group studies, the participants are shown an actual product or series of products. They're asked to provide their honest opinion about the products. They may be asked about the products' design or packaging. If the product can be used or sampled in a focus group setting, the participants may be invited to try the product. For example, if you wanted to get kids' opinions about a new line of toys, you could bring in a group of children and invite them to actually play with the toys.

For a focus group to work you need participants who might reasonably be expected to use your product. If you want information on a new line of toys, it won't help you much to bring 80-year-olds into your focus group (unless you're wanting to find out how appealing the toys are to grandparents). You also need the facilitator to have some skill so that the session stays on track. If the people in the focus group session start talking about something unrelated to your product, the facilitator needs to step in and gently guide them back to the topic at hand.

For a new jewelry company, the company founder could invite in a few people for a focus group. It would be best if the founder picked people who aren't her close friends. Friends sometimes tell us what they think we want to hear rather than the truth. If the company founder wants to find out about the true appeal of her jewelry, she needs focus group participates who are willing to be objective. She could ask some classmates who aren't close friends, or she could ask her friends' cousins to participate, for example.

When she gathers her participants together she can begin by asking them some basic questions about their jewelry buying habits. Then she could show some samples of her jewelry and ask for honest feedback. As you can imagine, a focus group session will give you information you can't get through written or online surveys. In a focus group session you can observe the participants' facial expressions, tone of voice, and so forth. If they're bored by your product, you'll pick up on that in a focus group session. Sometimes participants in a focus group will offer good ideas. For example, they may think of a different way to package the good, or they may come up with another variation of the good. Be open to the feedback you receive in a focus group session, but also keep in mind that you're just getting the opinions of a few people. That's one of the downsides of a focus group study. You only get information from a few potential consumers. A survey offers you the opportunity to gather information from a lot more people. The more people you survey, the better your information will be. As a general rule you want to survey at least 30 people, and it's best if you survey people you don't know (or don't know well). If you have the time and resources to survey more than 30 participants, then it's worthwhile to do so. More information and better information will make your business better and give you a greater chance at success.

$$

CHAPTER 8

Finding Money for Your Business

So you've come up with a great idea for a business. You've come up with a plan, or at least a partial plan, for your business. You've also done some research on your market. It sounds like you're ready to launch your business. The thing you're going to need at this point is money.

Of course, one of the reasons you're starting a business is because you want to *make* money. There's a saying that goes something like, "It takes money to make money," and there's definitely some truth to it. It takes money to start a business. How many money? That all depends on the kind of business you want to launch. Where are you supposed to get the money?

Finding money for business startups is what this chapter is all about. Following is a list of the most common sources of startup capital for budding entrepreneurs.

What is Capital?

Capital can mean several different things, depending on how the word is used. In business, *capital* most often means money. A lot of times capital refers to the money someone has invested in a business, or the money someone has available to invest in a business.

Common Sources of Startup Capital for a Business:

1. Your Own Savings

You may have some money saved up from your allowance or from birthday gifts. It's great if you already have enough money on hand to start your business. Some entrepreneurs work hard to earn the money they need to start their businesses. If you've put in some thought and come up with a solid business plan, you should have a good idea how much money you'll need to get started. Suppose you figure out that you need $500 to get your venture up and running. You could consider asking for money for your next birthday and/or asking your parents or caregivers if you could do some extra chores for money. If you focus on the goal of raising that amount of money, you may surprise yourself at how fast you reach it.

2. Friends and Family

What if the amount of money you need to launch your business is more than you can raise in a reasonable amount of time? That's actually the case for many entrepreneurs. They have a great idea, a great plan, and perhaps even a great team, but they lack the capital to get their idea off the ground. The first place many entrepreneurs look for additional funds is toward their family members and friends. If you have relatives or friends with money to lend, they may be willing to help you out. But keep in mind that things can get sticky later on if the business doesn't work out. If you borrow money from family members or friends, it's best to have a written agreement. Also, make sure you're not borrowing money that your friend or relative needs for living expenses.

3. Banks

Banks are a good source of startup capital. Banks make loans to people who want to buy houses and larger consumer goods like cars and boats. Banks also make loans to people who want to start businesses (and to businesses that have already been in operation for some time). It's not very likely that a bank will loan money to a kid who wants to start a business, but it's a source to keep in mind for the future.

Oftentimes when banks make loans they want to see some collateral. That may be sort of a big word, but it's not too difficult to understand what it means. **Collateral** is an asset, or something of value, that backs a loan. If a person borrowed money from a bank to buy a house, the house would be the collateral. If the person failed to pay back the loan, the bank would take the house—the collateral.

A bank will also look at a person's *credit history* when deciding whether or not to make a loan to that person. If you do a job good paying your bills on time, and especially paying back loans you've taken out, you'll have a good credit history. If you miss payments or make them late too often, you'll end up with a bad credit history. Every person is assigned a *credit score*, which is sort of like a grade on an exam, except the highest possible value is well over 100. Most people have a credit score in the 500 to 800 range. The higher your credit score, the better your credit history and the more likely banks are to loan you money for houses.

4. Partners

Another way to get startup capital for a business is take on a partner. A partner can contribute capital *and* effort to the business. Of course, that means the partner will be part owner of the business and will share in any profits the business earns.

It can feel lonely at times starting a business, so it can be useful to have someone else to talk to about the company's ups and downs. Launching a business also involves a lot of work, so it's helpful to have someone to share the burden. You should know that when you have a partner you give up some control over how the business operates. Your partner may not always see eye to eye with you. At times you'll have to compromise—but so will your partner. You've probably worked as part of a team before, and if you have you already know about disagreements and compromise.

There's nothing that says you're limited to only one business partner. You can have several business partners, with each of them contributing capital and effort to the business. It probably goes without saying that the more partners you have, the less control you'll have personally over the business.

What is a Silent Partner?

It is possible to have a business partner who only contributes money to the business and nothing else. Such a partner is typically known as a *silent partner*. Silent partners aren't expected to contribute effort to the business, and they usually don't have a say in how the business is operated. They contribute capital, and they are part owners. As a part owner, a silent partner does get to share in any profits the business earns.

5. Investors

We discussed investors in the last chapter. In that chapter we said that an investor is a person who uses his money to attempt to make more money. We also pointed out that people invest money in stocks, bonds, real estate, and many other things, including business startups.

Taking on an investor is a lot like taking on a business partner. Some investors will want to have a say in how the business operates, especially if they invest a lot of capital in the business. Other investors won't be very involved in the business operation, but they'll still expect a share of any profits the business generates. In such a case, an investor would be like a silent partner.

Investors who provide capital to business startups are often referred to as *venture capitalists*. Wealthy individuals who are willing to fund startups in the very early stage are sometimes call *angel investors* or *business angels*.

6. Crowdfunding

Crowdfunding has been a real innovation in the startup world. It's changed the way many entrepreneurs approach the process of raising capital. When a business uses crowdfunding, it raises money from lots and lots of contributors. Usually each contributor puts in a very small amount.

Suppose you need $10,000 to start your company. You could get two investors to each put $5,000 into your business—that would be a more traditional way of going about it. Crowdfunding works differently. With crowdfunding you could get 500 people to each put $20 into your business, or maybe you could get 1,000 people to each put $10 into your business.

Sometimes the contributors to a crowdfunding campaign may get small shares of ownership in the company they've given money to. A more common practice is for crowdfunding contributors to receive some kind of reward, such as a sample of the company's product, a T-shirt, or some other prize.

Most crowdfunding happens on the Internet. Kickstarter and Indiegogo are two of the better-known crowdfunding sites. If you visit those sites, you'll find instructions for setting up a crowdfunding campaign. Crowdfunding is definitely worth consideration as a source for startup capital, especially if you're pretty handy with social media.

7. Grants

A grant is like a loan with one big difference: you never have to pay it back. That's right! A grant is free money for your business. Most grants come from the government, or from non-profit organizations. Some corporations also offer grants.

Not every entrepreneur will be able to get a grant. Competition for available grants can be fierce, since it's money that never has to be paid back. But it's certainly worth your time to find out if there are any grants you may qualify for. There are special grants available to minority-owned businesses, female-owned businesses, single moms getting into business, and businesses that are located in underserved areas (i.e., places where a lot of poor people live). Do an Internet search on "business grants" and see what you come up with. Be sure to try variations on your search. For example, you can include the city or county or state where you live after the term "business grants." You can also try a search that includes the type of business you're aiming to start.

8. Contests

Contests are another source of free money for business startups. We're not talking about the lottery here. What we're talking about are contests set up especially for entrepreneurs. Sometimes referred to as pitch competitions or elevator pitch competitions, many of these contests involve entrepreneurs presenting their business concepts before judging panels. Awards are typically given to the business concepts that have the greatest chance of success, at least in the eyes of the judges. Many such contests are sponsored by colleges, and some are open to the community at large. Do a search on "business pitch competitions" or "startup competitions" in your area and see what you find out. It would also be worth your time to contact the business departments of any colleges in your area and ask if they are hosting any startup competitions, or if they know of any nearby.

From here on out, it will be useful for us to assume that you actually got the business—*While Ur Away Home Pet Care*—up and running. Maybe you started the business with the birthday money you've been saving up for the past three years. Maybe you won a startup contest, or you completed a successful crowdfunding campaign. However it happened, we'll assume that you launched the business and now it's a reality. You, for the sake of argument, are a proud business owner! We'll spend the rest of this book examining some topics related to the operation of your brand new business. Starting a business is one thing, but keeping it going—and making it successful—is a whole other matter.

$$

CHAPTER 9
Promoting Your Business

As mentioned in an earlier chapter, advertising and promotions is a very important part of marketing. If you have a great product, but no one knows about it, you won't be in business long. Everyone knows what advertising is—we're all bombarded by ads all day long. What most people don't know is that a lot of thought goes into creating those ads. There are a lot of decisions to be made with regards to advertising. How do you decide what types of advertising would work best for your business? How often should you advertise your product? And how do you cut through the clutter (all those other ads) so that people actually hear your message?

In this chapter we'll discuss different kinds of ads and the pros and cons of each. We'll also discuss public relations, which is related to advertising and promotions.

Why Advertise?

Is it really necessary for a business to promote itself? If you have a really good product, won't people find out about it on their own? Aren't some businesses already famous enough that they can stop advertising?

Of course, it's always possible that people will find out about your product some other way besides through advertising. Friends will tell friends about businesses and products they like a lot. That's the best form of advertising because it doesn't cost the business a cent. Also, a person is more likely to believe what a friend tells her than what she hears in an ad. That form of advertising is called word-of-mouth advertising. You can't buy it from a TV or radio station or newspaper, but a smart businessperson will try to encourage it. We'll discuss some ways you might encourage word-of-mouth advertising later in the chapter, in the section on public relations.

What about the question of certain businesses already being so famous they don't need to advertise? Think about well-known companies like McDonald's, Pepsi, and Nike. Everyone knows about them, right? Yet those companies, and hundreds of other very well-known companies, continue to advertise. There are reasons they continue to advertise. If you study the history of American business, you'll find that some very large—and very famous—companies have closed down over the years. Just because a company becomes large and well-known it doesn't guarantee that the company will be on top forever. The business world is highly competitive. Consumers have lots of choices, lots of different ways they can spend their hard-earned dollars. If a company decided not to advertise, it would be allowing its competitors to gain an advantage. If Pepsi stopped advertising, Coke would have an opportunity to grab a bigger share of the cola-drinking market (and vice versa).

Having said all that, it's also important to note that all forms of advertising aren't the same. Some types of advertising are better suited for certain products. In other words, if a company had, say, $1,000 to spend on advertising in a given month, the company wouldn't just randomly purchase $1,000 worth of ads. The company would carefully plan out how that money would be spent, so that it would get the biggest bang for its advertising dollar. A plan like this is often called an **advertising campaign**. Some companies hire advertising agencies to help them put together advertising campaigns. Advertising agencies know how to create different kinds of ads, and they have experts working for them who know which kinds of ads work best for various products.

There are at least several dozen forms of advertising and we don't have space in this book to cover them all. What follows is a list of the major types of advertising, along with the advantages and disadvantages of each.

Television Ads – TV ads are obviously the most visual form of advertising. A TV ad can relay a lot of information about your product in a short amount of time. TV advertising is generally one of the more expensive forms of advertising, and that is one its major disadvantages.

Radio Ads – Radio ads usually aren't expensive as TV ads, but they aren't cheap either. There's no visual element to radio ads, so they may not work as well for products that need to be seen. Another downside of radio advertising is that not as many people listen to the radio as in the past. Still, radio advertising can work well for certain types of local businesses, particularly when the businesses are promoted by local radio celebrities.

Newspaper Ads – As every year goes by, more and more people are reading their news online. Not nearly as many people read newspapers as in decades past. Young people are far less likely to read newspapers than older citizens. For that reason, businesses that cater to younger customers may want to consider other forms of advertising. Still, newspaper advertising may be very effective for certain types of businesses.

Magazine Ads – Ads in major magazines are very expensive, however, there are smaller regional and local magazines that are better suited for small business advertising. One good thing about magazines is that you can easily target people who are likely to be interested in your product. For example, a company that sells hunting knives should definitely consider running ads in hunting and outdoors magazines. It wouldn't make sense at all for a hunting knife company to run ads in beauty magazines.

Billboards/Outdoor Ads – Outdoor ads consist of more than just billboards. Signs on taxis, the sides of buses, bus stops, and benches can all be thought of as outdoor advertising. Outdoor ads make a lot of sense for businesses that are location specific. For example, a restaurant on the side of a particular highway may want a billboard to alert drivers that food is available. But the restaurant wouldn't likely want a billboard that's 400 miles away.

Direct Mail – Direct mail is mail that's sent to potential customers for marketing purposes. Some people call it "junk mail." In a way it is junk mail if it's sent to the wrong places, the wrong households. If an eighty-year-old grandfather gets an ad in his mailbox for sparkly fingernail polish, it could be considered junk. The fingernail polish company would not have done a good job putting together its mailing list. On the other hand, if the grandfather had received an ad featuring a delicious new kind of beef jerky, and beef jerky happened to be his favorite food treat, then he wouldn't consider the ad junk. The ad would be very useful to the grandfather because it would have alerted him to a product he'd likely enjoy. Direct mail can be very effective for small or large businesses if they carefully create their mailing lists.

Online Ads – The newest advertising medium is online advertising. Online ads come in several different forms. Some ads always appear on certain websites. Some ads are pop-up ads. Some ads are sent out via emails (like direct mail through the Internet). Social media also offers several advertising possibilities. One great advantage of online advertising is that it can be done in a very targeted manner. A company can easily reach the customers who are the most likely to be interested in their products. The disadvantages on online advertising are relatively few. If you're selling a product that appeals to very old consumers, then it's possible many of your potential customers aren't online much. You would want to use more traditional forms of media to reach those individuals. Also, online advertising changes faster than any other form of advertising, so more time must be set aside to learn about all of its ins and outs.

As we already pointed out, there are many other forms of advertising. For example, when you go to a movie theater, you usually see commercials play on the big screen before the movie starts. When you walk into the restroom at the movie theater you're bound to see advertisements on the walls. You may have had someone come to your door trying to sell you a coupon book. Those coupons are a type of advertising.

When a business is brand new it typically has to find inexpensive ways to get the word out about its products. For the While Ur Away pet sitting business, you would probably begin with flyers and ads on Internet bulletin board sites. Social media would also be a good way to let people know about the service. It's also usually a good idea to have some business cards printed up. You can keep some with you and hand them out to people you meet, especially people who are pet owners.

Logos and Slogans: Two Basic Branding Tools

Most businesses have logos and many also have slogans. You've seen thousands of logos. They're graphic designs, usually presented with the business name (though not always). Some logos are just made up of the business name with no other images or design elements. Typically logos that are just names have the letters printed in some interesting or unique font. Some logos have become very famous. If someone asked you to draw the logo for Nike, you'd probably be able to do so without giving it much thought.

Slogans are short verbal expressions that help get across some message about a company or its products. A car dealer might have the slogan "Great cars, even better prices." A bakery that sells pies might have the slogan "Pies the way grandma used to make them." A plumber might have the slogan "If we can't fix it, it ain't broke." Of course, your English teacher would tell you that last slogan contains some bad grammar, but slogans don't have to be

Logos and Slogans:
Two Basic Branding Tools (contd)

grammatically correct. The purpose of a slogan is to express something about your company or its products in as few words as possible. A slogan is also better if it's catchy and easy to remember. If it's something that easily sticks in people's heads, then it's a good slogan.

Logos and slogans are two basic tools companies use to brand themselves. A *brand* is to a company what a personality is to a person. Consumers get to know a company by its brand. Used together, logos and slogans can go a long way in creating impressions in the minds of consumers.

What kind of logo and slogan might you use for *While Ur Away Home Pet Care*? What kind of logo and slogan might you use for a business you're thinking of starting?

Public Relations

Public relations consists of the things a company does to create and maintain a positive image in the eyes of the public. It's another way to promote the company and its products. All companies like to receive favorable publicity, or media coverage. A company with a particularly unique or innovative product can quickly become known coast to coast through widespread publicity.

A great thing about publicity is that the company doesn't have to pay for it. It's like advertising, except that it's free. Another great thing about publicity is that people are more likely to believe it than they are ads. A news story about a company has more *credibility* than an advertisement because people know the company didn't pay for the news story.

Sometimes news reporters find out about interesting companies or products and decide on their own to write news stories about those companies and products. But there's nothing wrong with a company letting the media know what it's up to. A company can send out something called a press release. A press release is basically an announcement. It's not the same as a news story. It's sort of like the bare bones of a news story. When a company sends a press release to the media, the company hopes that reporters will be enticed to write a news story about the company. The press release includes the company's contact information so that reporters can call and interview the company's employees or owners.

Sending out press releases is part of a company's public relations strategy. Large companies even hire people to manage the firm's public relations, and to seek positive publicity for the company and its products. People like to talk about what's going on in the world. When a company gets good publicity, people are likely to talk about the company. ("Hey, man, have you heard about that new gizmo that does _____?") Good publicity can therefore create word-of-mouth advertising. And, as we mentioned earlier, word-of-mouth advertising is the absolute best form of advertising available to a company.

$$

CHAPTER 10
Keeping Track of It All

Once your business is up and running it's important for you to keep track of your business's finances. You need to know when money comes, how much comes in, and where it's coming from. You also need to keep tabs on how much money is being spent and what it's being spent on.

The process of keeping track of your business's finances is known as **accounting**. People who do such work professionally are called accountants.

It would take a long time to learn everything you need to know to be an accountant. This chapter won't teach you to be an accountant, but it will introduce you to a few basic accounting terms and concepts.

What is CPA?

Every industry has its own set of terms, and sometimes those terms are in abbreviation form. Terms in abbreviation form are sometimes called acronyms. You may already know that "NFL" stands for "National Football League." The abbreviation "NFL" is an acronym.

There are lots of acronyms in business. One acronym almost all businesspeople know is "CPA," which stands for "certified public accountant." That phrase may sound a little fancy, but it just refers to a person who has gone to school to learn accounting and has passed a test. The test proves that the person, the accountant, really knows his or her stuff.

Most businesses will hire a CPA, or maybe even several, to help with the accounting that needs to be done. There are a lot of complex rules in accounting, and many business owners feel that it's better to have an expert's help than to try to learn all the rules themselves.

Money Coming In and Money Going Out

Every business has money coming in and money going out, just like most people have money coming in and money going out. You probably do as well. If you earn an allowance, that's money that comes in to you. From that money, you may spend some of it on clothes, or video games, or books, or whatever. Of course, when you spend money on things you want to buy, that's money going out. **Cash flow** is what accountants call the money coming in and going out of a business. When a company has *positive cash flow,* it means that the business has more money coming in than going out. If a company has negative cash flow, then it has more money going out that coming in. When a company has a lot of cash, the company is said to have a lot of **liquidity**. That doesn't mean the company is all wet. It simply means that the company has in its possession a lot of cash or other things that can quickly be turned into cash. In the world of business and finance, something is liquid if it can quickly be turned into cash. Checking account deposits can quickly be turned into cash. For a checking account deposit to become cash, all one has to do is write a check and remove the money from the account. A building is usually not very liquid. To turn a building into cash, the building must be sold. It take can some time—maybe even a whole lot of time—to sell a building and get the cash. Companies typically like to have some liquidity so that they can easily pay their bills while also having money on hand in case emergencies arise.

Revenues

Money that comes into a business is called **revenue** or **income**. Actually revenue doesn't only come in the form of cash. Some businesses sell their products and services on credit, meaning that they allow their customers to pay for the goods later. Sales on credit still count as part of business's revenues (even though they're not part of a business's cash flows).

Many businesses have revenues coming from more than one source. Suppose a store—we'll call it Tony's TVs—sells a TV to a customer for $500. That $500 would be revenue for Tony's. Maybe Tony's also rents TVs to customers. If a customer pays $50 each month to rent a television from Tony's, that $50 would be part of Tony's monthly revenues. It may also be the case that Tony's offers repair services for televisions. If Tony's TVs fixes a customer's TV and charges $40 to do that, the $40 would also be part of the store's revenues.

Expenses

Expenses were defined in a previous chapter, but we'll spend some time on in here to make sure it's clear. We'll continue with the Tony's TV example. The money coming into the store includes money from selling TVs, from renting out TVs, and from repairing TVs. To offer those products and services, Tony's TVs will have to spend some money.

First of all, the store doesn't produce the televisions it sells. Tony's buys the TVs from a wholesaler, and it has to pay the wholesaler for the televisions. Suppose for a particular model of television—the one the store sells for $500—Tony's must pay a wholesaler $250. That $250 is part of Tony's **expenses**, which are also sometimes referred to as **expenditures**. This particular expense is called cost of goods sold. Tony's cost of goods sold may include more than just the television itself. For example, if Tony's puts all the TVs it sells into special super-strong boxes, the money the store spends on the boxes would also be part of cost of goods sold.

Wholesalers: Those Marvelous Middlemen

The term "wholesaler" might be new to you, but it's a very old concept. Consider a product like a shirt. Of course, lots of shirts are sold to consumers in retail stores, the kinds of stores you see in the mall. How did those shirts get onto the racks of those stores?

There may be some shirt makers that sell their shirts directly to retail stores, but most of the shirts were probably sold to the store by a wholesaler. A wholesaler is a middleman (or middlewoman) that buys the shirts from the shirt maker and resells them to the retail stores. The wholesaler might even buy shirts from lots of different shirt

Wholesalers: Those Marvelous Middlemen (contd)

makers and resell them to the stores. If the shirt-making factories are located in foreign countries then it's up to the wholesaler to ship the shirts to the country where the shirts will be sold in stores.

How does the wholesaler make money? By buying the shirts from the shirt maker for a low price and selling them to the stores for a higher price, the wholesaler can earn a nice profit. And you and your friends can have a nice selection of shirts to choose from on the store racks.

Tony's TV would have other expenses besides cost of goods sold. The store has to keep the electricity running, and it needs water for the bathrooms. The money the store pays the utility companies is part of an expense usually called utilities expense. Tony's TVs has to pay its workers (wages and salaries expense), pay for advertising (advertising expense), and pay for insurance (insurance expense). Those items are only examples. Most businesses have a lot of expenses. Any money a business owner has to spend to make the business run is part of the business's expenses. Note that not all expenses are paid in the form of cash. Tony's TVs may buy the TVs it's going to resell on credit, meaning that Tony's will pay the wholesaler for the TVs later. Even though Tony's TVs isn't forking over cash to the wholesaler right away, Tony's still records an expense when it purchases the TVs.

The Taxman Cometh . . .

According to an old saying, nothing in life is certain except for death and taxes. Households have to pay taxes, but so do business owners. Corporations must pay corporate tax. A sole proprietor has to pay income tax on the income from his or her business. Most retailers are required to collect sales taxes whenever customers purchase their products. The sales tax money is then sent to the local government. Some businesses also have to collect tourist taxes, or other similar taxes. Businesses owners also have to pay property tax on the assets—or property—they own.

The tax laws are complicated. For that reason, many business owners choose to hire CPAs to manage their taxes. If your business is really small, you may try to handle the tax paperwork yourself. But as your business grows, you'll definitely want to consider hiring a CPA to take care of all of that for you. The last thing a new entrepreneur needs is trouble with the taxman.

The "P" Word

A business owner wants to do his or her best to make revenues as high as possible and expenses as low as possible. That's just good common sense. You would prefer to have a greater amount of money coming into your piggy bank than flowing out of your piggy bank, right?

The difference between a company's revenues and expenses is known as *profit*, and it's a very important concept in business. Let's consider a simple example. Suppose Tony's TVs has $1,000,000 in revenues in a given year, and $800,000 in expenses in the same year. The store's profit for the year would be $200,000 (which is found by subtracting $800,000 from $1,000,000).

Is it ever possible for a company's expenses to be higher than its revenues? Businesses don't like it when that happens, but it can indeed happen. What if Tony's TVs only earned $700,000 in revenues in the same year it had expenses of $800,000? Its profit for the year would be -$100,000 (which is calculated by taking $700,000 minus $800,000). A negative profit is better known as a *loss*. It may go without saying that losses aren't good. Losses are a sign that business isn't going well. A company can usually handle having a loss every so often, but not on an ongoing basis. A company that experiences constant losses will eventually go out of business.

What are Assets and Liabilities?

If you study business long enough you're eventually going to come across the terms "assets" and "liabilities." An **asset** is something a company controls that is of value. Cash is an asset. Money in a bank account is an asset. A building is an asset, and so is a desk.

A **liability** is something a company owes or is responsible for paying in the future. A loan from a bank shows up as a liability for a company. Using an example mentioned earlier, a liability is created for Tony's TVs when the company buys TVs on credit from a wholesaler.

What are Assets and Liabilities? (contd)

Individuals and households also have assets and liabilities. You may not have any liabilities, but you certainly have assets. If you own a bicycle, that would count as an asset. If you have your own bank account, that would also be an asset. Take a few moments and see if you can list all of your current assets. Consider making another list of all the assets you would like to have in the future, when you're older.

Keeping Track of It All When You're Just Starting Out

So how do you handle all of this accounting stuff when you're just starting out? As we've already mentioned, the rules of accounting are complex, and people study them for years before becoming experts. That's why a grownup starting a new business usually hires an accountant to help out, unless the new entrepreneur already knows a lot about accounting. But as a kid starting a business, you may not be able to pay an accountant to help out.

In the beginning, your business will probably be fairly simple. You probably won't be selling your product on credit, or buying supplies on credit, or buying big things like buildings. You can begin by keeping careful records, either in a notebook or in a computer document or spreadsheet. Every time you make a sale, write down the amount in a column called "Sales" or "Revenue." Any time you pay for something for the business, write down the amount in a column called "Expenses."

If you have a few different kinds of expenses, then you should categorize them and keep a separate column for each in your notebook or spreadsheet. For example, if you have flyers printed up, you can include that under "Advertising Expense." If you run a lemonade stand and you spend money on cans on lemonade, you can include that under "Supplies Expense."

Every so often, add up the columns and subtract the expenses from the revenues. Hopefully your revenues are bigger than your expenses and you're earning a profit. If your profit is bigger than what you expected, you'll want to let your parents know about it. Your parents may agree that the business is making enough money that it makes sense to hire an accountant—especially if tax season is approaching!

$$

CHAPTER 11
Facing (and Overcoming) Business Challenges

Once you get your business up and running, your challenges aren't over. Some businesses get off to a great start, but end up stumbling when they face the first major hurdle. Keeping the business alive and keeping it growing is a lot like nurturing a garden. It takes constant attention, hard work, and dedication to make a small business grow into a bigger one. There's no way to predict what challenges any business will face, but this chapter outlines some of the difficulties commonly encountered by new entrepreneurs.

Challenge #1: Lack of Sales

One of the more disheartening challenges faced by new business owners is too little demand for their products and services. You've created a great product, or you've discovered a great product to resell, and you want everyone in the world to be as excited about it as you are. When people aren't buying as many of your products as you hoped, things can get pretty desperate pretty fast. Morale can suffer. The bills can start stacking up.

If sales aren't what you expected in the beginning, there's a good chance you didn't do enough market research before launching your business. What can you do if you find yourself in that situation? There's no one correct solution, but there are some potential solutions an entrepreneur can try. First, you can rework your marketing plan and/or put more resources into marketing. Perhaps you haven't correctly identified your target market. There may be lots of people who would love your product, and you just haven't found them yet.

Another possible solution is to work harder on sales. Maybe your advertising is doing a good job bringing people in. They're checking out your product, but they're not actually buying it. It may be the case that you need to hone your sales pitch. There are many excellent books and courses that teach sales skills. If people are stopping into your store or visiting your website but they're not biting, then work on finding ways to close the deal.

Of course, there may be an issue with your product. If the product doesn't meet customers' needs, then you may need to work on improving it. Sometimes a slight change can make all the difference. If there's no way to improve your product, then you may want to consider offering a different, related product.

Challenge #2: Undercapitalization

That's kind of a big word—"undercapitalization." It has a pretty simple meaning. It means that the business doesn't have all the money it needs. Sometimes a business is on the path to being successful, but it needs more money to get to the next level. For example, what if a new company gets a huge order for its product. That can happen if a large retailer like Wal-Mart or Target decides that it likes a company's product and wants to carry the product in all of its stores. In order to produce a large quantity to satisfy a big order, a company will need a lot of cash. Without that cash—that *capital*—the company is stuck between a proverbial rock and a hard place. If it can't find the money it needs, the company can't fulfill the big order and thus risks losing sales. A company in this situation will have to borrow the money it needs from a bank or else find an investor. Some companies fail not because they have a bad product or bad management, but because they can't find the money they need to expand.

Challenge #3: Too Many Chiefs

The "too many chiefs" problem usually happens in businesses that are organized as partnerships. What we're really talking about here is the problem of too many bosses, too many people in charge. If the partners in a partnership don't have clearly defined roles, they are likely to encounter problems. Some work may duplicated while other work doesn't get done. Partners may argue about how things are going to be done. Employees may find themselves confused, uncertain of whom to report.

In a partnership situation, it's a good idea for the roles and responsibilities of each partner to be written down. It's also a good idea for business partners to have a process in place for settling disagreements.

Challenge #4: Too Much Competition

Ideally you would have figured out who your main competitors are while researching your business and while putting together your business plan. But it's possible that after launching you might discover additional competitors you weren't aware of beforehand. It's also possible that new competitors may come along after you open your doors, particularly if you're successful. Successful businesses can expect to face competition.

When competition rears its head, the only thing an entrepreneur can do is work harder to provide better products at the best prices, and to offer the best customer service possible. Competition doesn't have to kill your business. Competition can actually make your business better if you maintain a good attitude about it.

Challenge #5: Employee Problems

A majority of businesses start without any employees. Usually it's the owner, or owners, slaving away, doing all the work themselves. But as a business begins to grow, it may become necessary to hire employees. When a business begins to hire employees, challenges are sure to appear.

One major challenge is finding good employees in the first place. You might think it would be easy; you just post an ad online and the resumes begin pouring in. You might get lucky and find someone good right away. But more than likely you're going to have to sift through a lot of applications and interview a number of candidates before finding people who'll fit well into your business.

Even after you find good employees, you'll face the challenge of training them and keeping them motivated. What happens when you have employees who don't do their jobs well? Firing workers is a tricky thing, and although sometimes it needs to happen, most managers find that it's not easy to do.

And, of course, many employees won't stick around in your business forever. They'll eventually move on, and then you'll have to repeat the whole process of hiring, training, motivating, etc. Like all things in life, though, the more practice you get managing people, the better you'll get at it.

Challenge #6: Too Much Success Too Quickly

How can a business possibly experience too much success? Isn't success exactly what all business owners are going for? Of course, all entrepreneurs want to be successful, but when too much success comes too quickly, it can actually be as much of a curse as it is a blessing.

Consider a new company that manufactures birdhouses and has enough supplies on hand to produce 1,000 birdhouses. Suppose the company's birdhouses are far more popular, more in demand, than expected. Suppose customers order 100,000 birdhouses through the company's online store. Now the company has a big challenge on its hands. First, the company will have to come up with a lot more supplies. Second, the company may have to hire more employees, or at least bring in some temporary employees, to produce the birdhouses. Also, what if the company's factory or production space isn't very big? What if the company can only produce 100 birdhouses per day given the size of its factory? Even if it bought more supplies and hired more employees, the company would need 1,000 days—well over two and a half years—to fulfill the order. And, of course, new customers would be placing new orders while the company struggles to fulfill the initial 100,000-unit

order. The company could find a bigger building, a larger production space, but that usually takes time. Companies usually
sign leases on their buildings, and a lease can lock a company
into a space for three years or more.

Considering all of this, can you see why too much success
too quickly can create problems for a new company? Maybe it's
not the worst problem a business can face, but some entrepreneurs have failed because they didn't manage their growth well.
Having said that, most business owners would much rather
face this challenge than the challenge of sluggish sales.

What is a Lease?

A **lease** is a special kind of agreement or contract. It's
a contract between a person renting a building or space
from another person. A person who rents an apartment
typically signs a lease. The lease states what the amount
of rent will be and when it will be due. The lease also
states the number of months or years the renter will
live in the apartment. There are likely other terms in
the lease as well. Is the renter allowed to have a pet
or not? Is the renter allowed to rent out a room in the
apartment to another renter? That would all be spelled
out in the lease.

Leases aren't just for apartments. Businesses also sign
leases for buildings, for offices, for store spaces, and for
other spaces. Leases on business spaces (sometimes
known as *commercial property*) typically cover longer peri-
ods of time.

Starting a new business is one of the most exciting things a person can do. It's like an adventure story in which the hero journeys through a magical land. The hero will surely face challenges, some of them quite large. But the hero always learns and grows because of the challenges. The hero may not know where she will end up, but she knows that she must keep moving forward. Of course, she may not make is far as she wanted to go—she could even make a wrong turn and end up getting lost. But it's also possible that she'll find riches bigger and grander than she ever imagined. She may even become the queen of her own "queendom" one day.

You must be courageous to be an entrepreneur. You won't encounter real dragons, but you'll certainly face other kinds of dragons (competitors, taxes, government regulations, etc.). At the start of your journey, you won't know everything you need to know. That's just fine. You'll learn along the way. As you progress on your entrepreneurial journey, you'll grow . . . not just as a businessperson, but also as a person in general. And like the hero mentioned in the little story here, you may find yourself rewarded one day beyond anything you've ever dreamed of.

It's happened for lots of others in our society. It can happen for you if you're brave enough to take the first step. Then the second step. Then the third, and so on.

$$

APPENDIX:
Sample Business Plan

While Ur Away
Home Pet Care
Business Plan

Company Overview

While Ur Away offers mobile, in-home pet sitting services. We travel to our customers' homes while they're away and take care of their pets. In addition to feeding the pets, we'll clean up any messes the animals make, and give them some attention. As a courtesy, we'll also bring in the mail.

We offer our services primarily within the city limits of Smithton. We also offer services outside the city limits (an additional per-mile charge will apply outside the city limits).

We offer our customers a free initial consultation, during which time we'll meet the customer and his or her pets. During this time we'll record any important information about the pets and their routines.

According to our analysis, a market exists for in-home pet care in Smithton and the surrounding area. Currently there are no professional branded companies in the area providing such services. As the first in the region, we hope to capture a large share of the in-home pet care market. We believe the company can be launched with a relatively small upfront capital investment, and we expect the company to be profitable in the first year.

Mission Statement

Our mission is to ensure the safety and well-being of our customers' pets so that our customers can enjoy some peace of mind while they're away from home.

Organization and Team

While Ur Away's founder and proprietor is Kylie Jones. Although Kylie is an 8th grader at Central Junior High School, she has several years experience as a pet sitter. She has taken care of dogs, cats, bunnies, hamsters, fish, birds, lizards, and a boa constrictor. Kylie has read over 50 books related to animal care, and she volunteers regularly at Smithton Bird Sanctuary. Her favorite subject in school is biology, and she intends to study veterinary medicine in college.

Sarah Jones, Kylie's older sister, will serve as *While Ur Away*'s second-in-command. Sarah, an 11th grader at Smithton High School, brings her experience as a graphic designer to the business. In addition to graphic design, Sarah is a social media expert. Sarah will be in charge of *While Ur Away*'s marketing efforts, and she'll also provide transportation support (she's had her driver's license for over a year and she has her own car). In addition, Sarah, who's also worked as a part-time pet sitter, will assist Kylie with pet care duties.

Services

Basic Drop-in Visits

Our basic service at *While Ur Away* consists of drop-in visits to our customers' homes. During each visit, a *While Ur Away* care ambassador will bring in the customers' mail (unless the customer requests otherwise), leave food and water for the customers' pets, clean up any messes the pets have made, and give the pets some attention. If the pets are dogs, our care ambassador will take them out for a brief walk. Our basic drop-in visit ranges from 15- to 19-minutes in length. We can drop in once per day, every other day, or as requested by the customer. The fee for our basic drop-in visit is $20 per visit. We will offer our customers discounts if they order five or more drop-in visits and pay for them in advance.

Extended Visits

While Ur Away also offers extended visits. Our extended visits include all the same elements of our basic drop-in visits, except that our care ambassadors spend additional time with the pets, walking them (dogs only) or giving them extra attention. Our extended visits are one-hour in length. The fee for our extended visits is $38 per one-hour visit.

Live-In Pet Care (House and Pet Sitting)

During the summer months, *While Ur Away* offers live-in pet care services. A *While Ur Away* care ambassador will actually stay at the customers' home, offering almost constant care for the customers' pets while also keeping the house in order. The fee for our live-in pet care service will be set on a case-by-case basis.

The Market

According to a 2015-2016 survey by the American Pet Products Association (APPA), 65 percent of American families own a pet. According to the latest census data, roughly 40,000 families live in Smithton and the surrounding area. That means there are 26,000 total potential customers for *While Ur Away*'s services. Not all of those families will go on vacation, but even if half of them do that still leaves 13,000 families that might potentially need pet sitting services. If just 5 percent of those 13,000 families use our services one week per year, that would be 650 families per year. Assuming each of those families paid for three drop-in visits for the week they're gone, *While Ur Away* would earn $60 per family per year, making our total revenues $39,000 for the first year.

It's possible that *While Ur Away* will capture more than 5 percent of the market, in which case our revenues will be higher than $39,000. It's also likely that some families will want to purchase our extended visits or our live-in pet care services, which would increase our revenues by an even greater amount.

Competitive Environment

There is one doggy daycare in Smithton—Dino's Doggy Daycare. Dino's has been in operation for nearly 10 years, but so far it has never offered in-home pet care services. Some pet owners may prefer to leave their pets in a daycare away from home. However, according to the results of our surveys, more than 60 percent of pet owners would prefer to keep their pets at home while they're away. We know we can't compete with Dino's in the doggy daycare business; we don't have the facilities to offer that kind of service. But since Dino's doesn't offer in-home pet care services, we don't view the doggy daycare as a direct competitor.

There are a few individuals in and around Smithton who offer in-home pet sitting services, but so far there are no professional branded businesses offering such services. *While Ur Away* aims to be the first branded mobile, in-home pet sitting company in the Smithton area. We aim to build our brand image in such a way that it represents quality and professionalism in the minds of Smithton pet owners.

Marketing Plan

While Ur Away's marketing strategy has three basic parts.

First, we will produce colorful flyers with our logo and post them on bulletin boards throughout Smithton. We will also seek permission from veterinarians in the area to leave our flyers in their offices.

Second, we'll post ads on various online bulletin boards and send the word through social media that we're offering services in Smithton.

Third, we've identified a local magazine with affordable advertising rates that is geared toward middle- and higher-income families. We'll run an ad in the magazine's May edition and follow up with similar ads throughout the summer months.

To begin building our brand, all of our ads will feature our logo (which was designed by Sarah). We are still working on our slogan. We intend to test a few different potential slogans before settling on the final one we'll use in our marketing.

Operation Plan

In the beginning, all *While Ur Away* services will be provided by Kylie and Sarah. Kylie will handle all the customers that live within biking distance (approx. 5 miles) of the company's Smithton headquarters (301 Applegate Lane). Sarah will handle all other Smithton customers, along with those that live outside the Smithton city limits.

As demand for the company's services increases, additional employees will be hired. Employees will be paid minimum wage to start out. The company will be careful to only hire animal lovers. Bonuses will be offered to employees who provide excellent customer service, and to employees who refer new customers to our services. We will also experiment with a bonus referral plan for customers who refer other customers to our services (e.g., a free drop-in visit for anyone referring a friend or relative).

It's expected that much of the demand for our services will occur in the summer months, which is when Kylie and Sarah are most available. Our goal is to secure 12 to 18 drop-in visits per day, along with one or two extended visits per day, in the weeks between Memorial Day and Labor Day. We have already purchased a large map of the city. Along with the map, we'll use a GPS app to chart the shortest routes between our customers' homes so that we spend as little time traveling as possible. Ideally we will be able to complete an average of 2.5 drop-in visits per hour, which represents $50 in revenue for the company per hour worked.

Financial Plan

Projected Revenues and Expenses

As stated above, we are projecting revenues of $39,000 for our first year of operation. We don't expect to hire any employees the first year, so there would not be any expense for wages. We plan to spend $2,000 for marketing our first year. We are budgeting $3,000 for gas and for wear and tear on Sarah's car. We're also budgeting $400 for office supplies and another $200 for a business license and other fees. Since *While Ur Away* will operate out of Kylie's bedroom, there won't be any expenses for utilities or Internet service. With projected revenues of $39,000 for the first year and projected expenses of $5,600 for the first year, *While Ur Away* is projecting to earn a profit of $33,400 the first year (before taxes). The company will likely hire an accountant to complete the yearly statements and the tax forms, so this expense will also be subtracted from that amount.

Startup Costs

While Ur Away doesn't need the entire $5,600 to get started. The company will need to pay for a city business license.

Additionally, we'll need to purchase some office supplies and pay for some printing. All together the company—operating as described in this business plan—may be launched for $500. The remainder of the projected first-year expenses can be covered from the company's revenues.

$$ Notes

$$ Notes

$$ Notes

$$ Notes

$$ Notes

$$ Notes

$$ Notes

$$ Notes

$$ Notes

$$
Notes

www.ingramcontent.com/pod-product-compliance
Lightning Source LLC
Chambersburg PA
CBHW060624210326
41520CB00010B/1464